Pigs

PIGS

Art, Legend, History

Franco Bonera

Series editor: Giorgio Coppin

The Bulfinch Library of Collectibles

A Bulfinch Press Book
Little, Brown and Company
Boston · Toronto · London

First North American Edition

English translation by John Gilbert
Series editor: Giorgio Coppin

ISBN 0–8212–1873–5
Library of Congress Catalog Card Number 91–55249
Library of Congress Cataloging-in-Publication information is available.

Bulfinch Press is an imprint and trademark of Little, Brown and Company (Inc.)
Published simultaneously in Canada by Little, Brown & Company (Canada) Limited

PRINTED IN ITALY

CONTENTS

Virtue's reward: better dead than alive

It is about time that we admitted it: no animal on Earth is more unjustly treated than the pig. Abused, mocked, insulted, vilified, exploited – and, in the end, slaughtered. And by whom? By those, of course, who should be morally obliged to regard it as the best of all their animal friends: men. Instead, since time immemorial man has scorned this fat four-legged beast, considering it unworthy of any particular consideration. Naturally, man will claim that he loves the creature, sometimes even to excess: but, in truth, he only loves it dead.

It may perhaps be argued that many other great figures in history have suffered the same bitter fate and been consigned to the afterworld before being fully and deservedly appreciated. Indeed, back in 1665, a gastronome from Bologna named Vincenzo Tanara remarked that "the pig may be compared to those virtuous individuals who are treated badly during their lifetime but who, when they are dead, are missed and honoured, and fortunate are those who have their writings or books." But this kind of philosophical reflection hardly makes the fate of the poor pig any less

An Italian craftsman emphasizes the
corpulent but also the handsome
characteristics of the pig. Opposite: a pig in
the shape of a golf ball, with a silver head
and tail.

cruel or atrocious, because it is one thing to go to one's Creator in the proud certainty of leaving down below the fruits of a talent or an art that only those who come later will be able to appreciate, and quite another matter to depart this life aware that one's own mortal remains are going to make those still alive happy, filling their stomachs and eliciting their applause. If we accorded the pig even the slightest measure of respect while it was alive, perhaps even its supreme sacrifice might somehow be less painful. Instead, we persist in calling it all the names under the sun, perpetuating an oral and written tradition whose origins are lost in the mists of time, because from Adam onwards the pig has been condemned unanimously as one of the ugliest creatures in the world.

As evidence of this attitude, compare two texts, published seventeen centuries apart. In A.D. 77 Pliny the Elder, compiling his *Natural History*, proclaimed that the pig was "the most stupid of animals." In 1788 Georges Louis Leclerc, Comte de Buffon, sending to the printers a work bearing the same name as that of Pliny, made matters worse by stating that "of all quadrupeds, the pig seems to be the ugliest animal; its imperfections of form appear to influence its nature; all its habits are clumsy, all its tastes are filthy; all its feelings amount to no more than violent lust and brutal greed which make it devour indiscriminately anything it

The brush stuck into the brass container is made of pig bristles: the object was made at Bruges, in Belgium, early in the twentieth century.

happens to find." These are just two of the innumerable examples of how the pig has been defamed in print down the centuries. Therefore, it is easy to understand why, from every point of view, comparing your nearest and dearest to a pig is regarded as the worst of insults. Both "pig" and "swine" are often used as forms of insult. The gravity of the offence can vary but, broadly speaking, if you call anyone a pig you are accusing them of the worst physical and moral level to which the human race can sink, without for a moment pausing to consider whether the pig itself is really guilty of such base instincts and behaviour.

The unfortunate pig is credited with no positive qualities and virtues, so that anyone going so far as to challenge the denigrating opinions of Pliny and Buffon, describing, say, a gifted student as "intelligent as a pig," would be condemned as mad. Yet the truth is – as has been shown by research – that the pig is far from stupid. Indeed, as far as brain

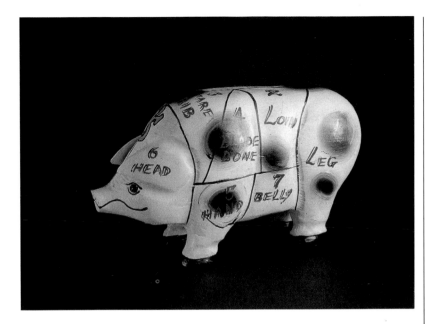

This wooden model of a pig from a butcher in Dallas, Texas, has its body neatly divided into cuts, with prices per pound shown.

function is concerned, it far outranks all other farm animals in intelligence, and may even be compared with mammals such as dolphins and dogs, acknowledged to have mental skills second only to humans. It might be more to the point to describe an altruistic person as "generous as a pig," for that is a quality truly applicable to the creature. This generosity, however, is a living virtue that the pig can only exercise posthumously, as explained by a strange document of medieval origin entitled *The Testament of a Pig*, based on an older Latin text, ostensibly written by a pig, and known to children in ancient Rome as a kind of nursery rhyme. The pig, aware of its impending fate, makes a last will and testament before facing the executioner. He leaves his snout to the farmer, to help him look for truffles; his trotters to the stationer, who can use them for flattening sheets of paper; bristles to the shoemaker, for making shoelaces; softer hairs to the painter, for making brushes; the bladder to the boy, who can blow it up into a balloon; his milk to the girl, who will drink it and stay healthy; his skin to the miller, who can use it to make sacks for flour; the rind to the modeller and the chemist, who will change it into glue and soap; tallow to the candlemaker, who will mix it with that of the ox and the goat; lard to the weaver, who uses it for tanning the hemp; his bones to the gambler, who can make new dice from them; bile to the traveller, for removing thorns from his feet; nails to the gardener, for fertilizing the ground; and his tail to the alchemist, so that he realizes he will reap the same reward from all his activities as the pig did from wagging it day in, day out. And naturally, his flesh to a crowd of gluttons who will serve it up in various ways and fill their bellies with it.

Although our industrial civilization would hardly use many of these by-products for the original purposes intended, there is no denying that this is true generosity. There is actually a saying that when a pig is slaughtered only the squeal is lost, and indeed practically all the carcass has some commercial use. Yet if we were to be informed by the family lawyer that we had been left a fortune by an elderly aunt, we would hardly praise her magnanimity by exclaiming that she was treating us like an old pig.

Imagine, too, a girl who has to endure a long separation from her fiancé and who swears eternal devotion to her loved one by whispering: "Darling, I shall be as faithful to you as a pig!" This tender promise may lead to misunderstanding, and perhaps worse, if the young man happens not to have read a passage written by an Englishman named Hyams, who, on the basis of personal experience, boasts that his farmyard pigs show an attachment and liking for human beings that verges on devotion. So they are faithful, too; not to mention obliging,

since they seem happy to adapt themselves to all kinds of different duties. Such tasks may range from hunting for truffles to taking over unexpectedly as beasts of burden, as was demonstrated in the nineteenth century by four obedient piglets from St Albans in Hertfordshire, who every morning drew the carriage of their proud and somewhat unconventional master to market. Another anecdote from the Victorian era tells how a certain Sir Henry Mildmay transformed his huge sow, named Slut, into a hunting companion more effective than a pointer. Apparently, within the short space of a week, Slut was able to flush various types of game such as partridges, pheasants, woodcock and rabbits; and whenever her master summoned her to go hunting, she would bound after him as excitedly as any dog at the sight of a gun.

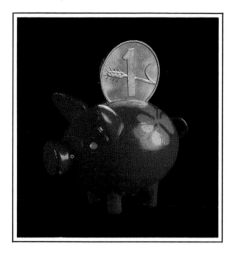

A wooden pig from Switzerland in the form
of a money box and thus a bringer of fortune.
Opposite: a mechanical pig with cooking
skills, from the 1950s.

The pig is quite a performer, too; given suitable training, it can take its place, unlikely as it may seem, alongside dogs and seals in the circus ring. There are reports, for example, of pigs happily entertaining the public in the arenas of ancient Rome, a tradition that was continued in fifteenth-century France and, even to the present day in Russia where the pig vies for center stage with star performers such as horses and monkeys.

All evidence points to the fact that the pig, given the opportunity, could prove itself as devoted a friend of man as the trusty dog. And maybe back in the beginning that was indeed its deservedly official role. In China there is a legend that, were it true, would represent a fundamental and dramatic turning point in the long history of the pig. There was once a little boy named Bo-Bo whose play companion was a very gentle and affectionate pig. At that time human beings did not feed on pig flesh, nor were pigs deliberately fattened up for slaughter; they were fairly small animals, valued for their lovable nature and particularly popular as

pets for children. So Bo-Bo's plump little friend enjoyed all the advantages that are today lavished on puppies. He played with his young master, wagged his tail happily and, when Bo-Bo ordered him to "play dead," he lay down at the boy's feet and did not move until he received a new command.

One awful day, however, when Bo-Bo's parents were working in the fields, and the youngster was alone with his pink playmate, the straw hut where the family lived caught fire. The boy, having rushed outside to safety, turned back with the noble intention of rescuing the animal as well. But the flames, which had spread quickly from the walls to the roof, prevented him from entering and there was clearly no way the pig could be saved. Once the fire was out and the smoke dispersed, Bo-Bo discovered the unfortunate creature, by now scorched and lifeless, and stretched out his hands to pick up his pet gently. But it was not to be: the moment he touched it, he was forced to drop the animal's body to the ground with a cry of pain, for it was still hot and had burned his fingers. To cool them, Bo-Bo instinctively put his fingers in his mouth. It was at that very moment that the fate of the race of pigs was sealed. In fact, according to the legend, the boy was so delighted with the taste of the roasted flesh on his fingers that he soon stopped crying, wiped away his tears, and sat down to console himself for his loss by feasting on the now-warm remains of his former friend. When his parents returned from the fields, they were astounded to find their house gone and even more amazed to discover their young son happy, full to bursting and uneffected by the disappearance of his playmate. After that, the word spread through all the neighbouring huts and villages, and everyone was eager to get a taste of the forbidden food, prepared to do away with those who had

only recently been their four-legged companions and finding unsuspected virtues in them, once dead. It was a catastrophic turn of events for the pig, who thereafter began to be reared and fattened solely for the purpose of being eaten. Indeed, the habit became so widespread that very soon the Chinese words for "flesh" and for "pig" were synonymous.

It was, therefore, because of the ungrateful Bo-Bo that the pig, once a friend, was demoted to the status of a food item, leaving the dog to wag its tail obediently at the feet of its master. From then on, the man of the house would return home daily to be greeted, not by hollow grunting but by joyous barking.

This, of course, is merely a legend, but suspicion that there might be some truth behind the story is given weight by the instinctive aversion – as any book on zoology or raiser of livestock will testify – that the pig shows towards the dog. It is as if the pig nurses some atavistic pang of jealousy, a sentiment, furthermore, typical of the two-legged race. In fact, the deeper we look the more it emerges that the pig has feelings that are not so very different, for better or worse, from our own. That may provide the psychological key to the scant regard that, away from the dinner table, we normally show for the poor pig. It is hard to imagine that pigs and humans could have anything else in common other than what is apparent from a casual inspection. The resemblance can be reduced, perhaps not insignificantly, to the common absence of fur and the presence, in many cases, of a pinkish complexion.

The pig is actually intelligent, sensitive, generous, loyal and jealous. Yet we judge the animal to be merely fat, filthy, stupid and disgusting. For this reason we condemn it as the most unworthy of creatures and accuse it of all the vices common to humankind. Thus, because nobody is without defects, anyone who at some stage departs from the straight and narrow will feel that he is "behaving like a pig," even if

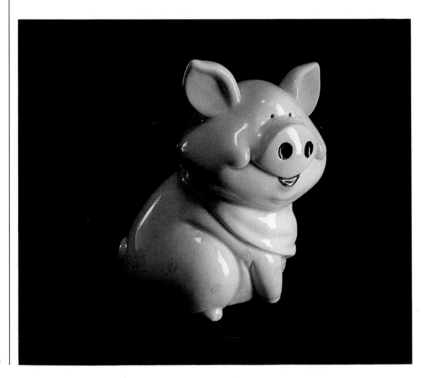

An aristocratic pig in human guise, made in England in 1956 and based on a Beatrix Potter drawing. Opposite: a smiling pig that, judging from its bib, is looking forward to a meal.

he lacks the courage to admit it. Abusing the pig becomes a painless way of recognizing our own faults without actually confessing to them. So the creature that is most like ourselves is deemed to be the worst of all animals. It is a transference mechanism similar to that whereby a primitive civilization would invent a so-called animal totem, the emblem of a clan or family with similar characteristics to those attributed to the animal. The more it is assumed that these qualities resemble one's own, the more one identifies with the animal, to the point of imagining it is one's direct ancestor. In the case of the pig, indeed, its transformation into a totem becomes an embarrassment, firstly because many cultures have now reduced it to the very opposite role, that of a taboo, and secondly because it is unthinkable that man should admit he is descended, albeit symbolically, from a pig, when he has hardly accepted the implication that he is related to the monkeys. In fact, there are those who, in the course of history, have shown no moral scruples in declaring themselves publicly to be the "children of the pig." Such is the case with the inhabitants of the New Hebrides, all of them descended, by their own admission, from a legendary clan chief born, at the beginning of time, to a sow.

The ancient Melanesians also believed that a mythical pig was the progenitor of their race and gave it credit for having founded one of the four classes into which their own society had, from the beginning, been divided. The Tibetans went even further and depicted the pig at the center of the Wheel of Existence, the originator of all things. In the latter instance, however, little merit was attached to the animal, for it occupied its central position as the very personification of the ignorance and passions of the Earth's inhabitants. Once again, we find the usual avalanche of insults, here elevated to cosmic proportions.

Peasants in many regions of France, up to the eighteenth century, were far kinder, addressing the pig, politely and graciously, as "monsieur," as if to atone for all the mischief and wickedness the creature had been forced to endure over the centuries. This title of respect served to underline, without any sense of shame, the similarities between man and beast. Indeed, three famous physicians of the past, from quite different periods and places, had shown a similar absence of prejudice when they concluded, independently, that the animal that most closely resembled humans was the pig; the discovery may not have filled them with joy, but all three were absolutely unswerving in their opinion. The scholars concerned were the Greek, Galen (A.D. 130–200), the Persian, Ibn Sina, better known as Avicenna (980–1037),

and the Spanish Jew, Moses Maimonides (1135–1204). Maimonides' bold assertion, made with extreme reluctance, was doubtless received with a good deal of hostility by many readers of his most famous work, an exposition of the Jewish faith entitled *Guide for the Perplexed*.

For others, however, such a comparison aroused feelings of horror. Surprisingly, one of these was the American writer, Edgar Allan Poe, whose stories were masterpieces of terror and nightmare. Poe's pessimism was based both on the similarity of the animal and human conditions, but even more by the indifference displayed by most people who traditionally visualize the pig merely as an animal to be butchered. His observation is shrewd and harsh, in as far as he sees a terrifying resemblance between human beings and their victims: he notes a depressing similarity between man's life on Earth and the arrogant confinement of the pig to its sty, between the sound of the dinner bell and the bang of the bucket, between a man snoring in an armchair and a pig grunting in the straw. And then, despite the likeness between the two, man kills the pig.

Yet some are more sympathetic, recognizing and accepting the resemblance. After all, it is one thing to brand one's fellow creature as a pig, but quite another to apply it to oneself and, moreover, proclaim it openly and defiantly. A notable champion was the Latin lyric poet Horatius Flaccus (Horace), who described himself proudly as "a shining pig from the herd of Epicurus." Even so, his pleasure-loving companions refused to take him seriously: they regarded his statement simply as poetic license.

Pigs from Japan: the one below, with its bewildered expression, is a nineteenth-century netsuke, *the traditional ivory toggle used for fixing the* inro, *a small lacquer box containing scent or medicines, to the belt; the three opposite are modern, two of them salt cellars and one a pepper pot.*

Someone up there dislikes me

Poor pig: spurned by man and even by God. Indeed, if we read the Bible carefully, it seems that the Creator, at some point, was convinced that this animal with its unlovely voice and flabby body was one of his more unsuccessful products. That could hardly have been a pleasant discovery, but the patient pig was probably not too surprised, given that from the very beginning it found itself caught up in the struggle between Good and Evil, placed first on the one side, then on the other, depending on human religious beliefs and superstitions. Most of the time man has put the creature on the wrong side of the fence, identifying it with Vice and loading it with shameful insults. And he has sought to justify such unworthy treatment by shifting the blame to God.

It is a complicated series of events, leading us inevitably to the biblical Mount Sinai, where Moses received from the Lord the Ten Commandments. Furthermore, Jehovah included among his holy laws a dietary code whereby the Jews were permitted to eat only the flesh of four-legged animals which conformed to two fundamental

requirements: a cloven hoof and the habit of chewing the cud. The pig, which is guilty of the former, but not the latter, is thus a forbidden food. Not only was it a forbidden food though, it was in no uncertain terms "unclean:" "Whatever parts the hoof and is cloven-footed and chews the cud, among the animals, you may eat. Nevertheless among those that chew the cud or part the hoof, you shall not eat these: The camel, because it chews the cud but does not part the hoof, is unclean to you. And the rock badger, because it chews the cud but does not part the hoof, is unclean to you. And the hare, because it chews the cud but does not part the hoof, is unclean to you. And the swine, because it parts the hoof and is cloven-footed but does not chew the cud, is unclean to you. Of their flesh you shall not eat, and their carcasses you shall not touch; they are unclean to you."

A dark, hairy boar, of Peruvian craftsmanship. Opposite: a white porcelain pig from Denmark. In ancient Egypt, the black pig was regarded as the incarnation of Evil, the white one as that of Good.

So far, so good, therefore, from the viewpoint of the pig, which is not yet destined to end up in the human stomach, and may perhaps be spared the attentions of slaughterers and butchers. A pity, then, that the All Powerful felt bound to add the command to consider the pig unclean. It was not just a matter of prohibiting the eating of pork chops and sausages but of outlawing the animal per se, so much so that from then on no observant Jew could even mention the pig, and the Talmud itself described it by the Hebrew phrase *davar aher*, another thing.

This divine ordinance was a harsh blow to the pig and his progeny, completely destroying its otherwise untarnished reputation. Looking at the story from the human point of view, much has been said and written concerning the motives that led the Children of Israel to condemn the innocent pig. There are two schools of thought: one suggests that the animal was ostracized for dietary reasons,

the flesh of the pig being too fatty for people living in hot regions, as well as on hygienic grounds, for they hoped, by proscribing it, to prevent the spread of parasitic diseases such as trichinosis and taeniasis, common among the neighbouring peoples. But, if this were true, it would not explain the presence of the pig in Palestine itself, where, even according to the sacred scriptures, the animal was normally reared.

In any event, this would not justify the divine curse: there are many other animals not eaten by man that are not automatically labelled unclean. So the second theory, which suggests that the moral ban stemmed from political motives, appears more probable. The pig, in fact, paid the price for the situation in the Middle East, which was already boiling up at the time of Moses. The Jews, fleeing from Egypt and anxious to forget the long, dark years of their enslavement along the Nile, were bent on distancing themselves from the customs and habits of their gaolers, and particularly from the religious rites which contravened their own unswerving brand of monotheism. And in the context of these rituals, the pig played an important part.

A polka-dot pig from Scotland. Opposite:
this pig with a crouched rider on its back is
Italian, a reproduction of a whistle found in
an ancient Apulian tomb.

In Egypt, the pig actually had two roles, contradictory to each other. It was the Egyptians who first devised the confused notions of the pig as a protagonist in the rift between Good and Evil. Having reflected deeply on the matter, they resolved the dilemma by creating a sexual distinction, ranging the sow on the side of the virtuous and relegating the male pig to the ranks of the sinners.

The great Egyptian goddess Nut, mother of heaven, was thus represented as a sow (though sometimes also as a cow), languidly reclining in the sky, busy suckling her piglets – the stars, and especially her favourite, a pig better nourished than his brothers – the Sun. Nut's maternal behaviour, nevertheless, was somewhat strange, for she swallowed her offspring at dawn and spat them out again at dusk, with the

exception of her special pet, the Sun, who dwelt in his mother's belly during the night and browsed in the sky by day.

Nut, therefore, was a beneficent creature, who received the sacrifices of all women on earth who wished for children and who had so far been unable to conceive.

Very different was the other pig in the Egyptian pantheon, a black male recognized by Pharaoh's subjects as the god Seth, the quintessence of evil. This divine pig had been guilty of a terrible crime, the killing of his brother Osiris, a noble individual worshipped by mortals as "the Benefactor." Not content with murdering him, the wicked, filthy swine cut up and ate the victim's body and then set out in search of his soul, with the ignoble intention of consuming it. Learning that the spirit of his good brother had found an eternal resting place in the Moon, he promptly began to devour that as well, without experiencing any digestive problems, seeing that, in common with all earthly representatives of his species, he was omnivorous. It was in this pig-like form, in the very act of devouring dear old Selene, that Seth came to be portrayed in the Egyptian temples dedicated to his cult, worshipped by those humans who, in the cosmic conflict between Good and Evil, had chosen to side with the latter.

So, on the banks of the Nile, the pig came to be considered a divinity in its dual guise, Nut the virtuous sow and Seth the wicked beast, both feeding on heavenly bodies. This saved the pig from the ravenous instincts of the human race, for it was hardly decent for a divine animal to end up on the dinner table of common mortals.

The priests, however, constituted a separate category and were therefore given certain special concessions. Because

Two versions of suckling sows: the acorn-shaped example below is of nineteenth-century Limoges porcelain, the one opposite, in marble powder, is modern.

*An unusual pig from Peru, represented as a
dentist, perhaps fashioned by someone
undergoing lengthy treatment. Following
double page: a wooden pig on wheels, made
in northern Italy.*

sacrifice played a part in their rites, a pig was offered once a
year to the unfortunate Osiris and the foresaken Moon, as
compensation for the moral injuries visited on them by the
pig, Seth. When the sacred ceremony was over, the
unhappy animal was cooked to a turn and sampled with
religious fervour by the priests, who had exclusive rights
to dispose of the remains.

They retained this right for the rest of the year, too,
telling the ordinary people that the pink creature could not
possibly be served up on their tables, without incurring
terrible divine punishment ranging from social castigation to
leprosy.

Even though the clergy were the only class permitted to
eat pork without risk of reprisal, this did not mean that the
animal, over and above its representation of Nut and Seth,
was unpopular with the Egyptians. Since they were unable
to consume it, the peasants of the Nile valley decided to
adopt it as a helper in the most important of their annual
tasks: sowing the crops. The farmer would ride his pig
across a field covered with the lime deposited by the great
river in flood, and the furrow traced in the soft ground by
the hooves of the animal would indicate the precise depth at
which the cereal would take root, with the promise of an
abundant harvest. Obviously, this specialized work, with its
vaguely divine associations, commended the pig to the
subjects of the Pharaoh, and allowed it, by and large, to lead
a fairly tranquil life, with the annual exception of that
notorious priestly banquet.

In western Asia, the pig had shown itself to be simply
more intelligent than the sheep or the camel, inasmuch as
neither by instinct or nature could it be induced to wander
around obediently in flocks and herds, or set off on
interminable treks through the desert: clearly it had no

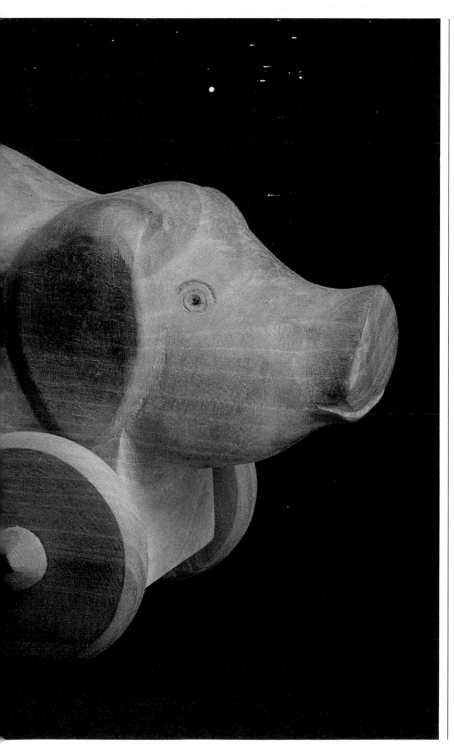

intention of travelling about in groups like a foolish ruminant. The people of western Asia, traditionally nomadic, were thus suspicious of it and were in agreement with the Jews that here was a creature to be shunned. So when Mahomet, in his teaching of the Koran, also condemned the pig as unclean, he was merely confirming and codifying a prejudice that was by now irreversible. He did not point out, however, that it was the pig that rejected the Arabs, and not vice versa, and he was thus guilty of the greatest injustice towards the animal. Although neither the Koran nor the Bible contain any justification for the ban, the Crusaders, when they reached the Holy Land, came across a legend which purported to explain it.

Mahomet announced one day to his disciples that Allah, wishing to reward the new faith, was about to send them a

mountain of cakes and honey. But when the pious Arabs

reached the spot where, according to the Prophet's
indications, the divine gift should have materialized, they
found, instead of the promised delicacies, a herd of fat pigs
which had got there first and had freely gobbled up the
whole lot. It was then that Mahomet, in his surprise and
anger, hurled his curse against all pigs, present and future.
Allowing for the fact that the Christians may have modified
the tale to suit their own purposes, maintaining that it was
not Allah but the Prophet himself who laid out the dainties
later devoured by the famished pigs, the substance of the
story remains unchanged, resulting in the banishment of the
creatures from the world of Islam as well.

No better fate awaited the pig in its dealings with
Hinduism and Buddhism. In the former case, the animal
was declared unclean, but for a very unusual reason: its sin,
according to Brahma, who had raised the cow to the status
of a god, was that it fed on refuse and was reared by the
humbler castes. Immoderate feeding habits and bad
company thus made the pig an undesirable individual, so
much so that if a Brahmin, a member of the highest priestly
caste, succumbed to sin, he would be punished by returning
as a pig in his next reincarnation.

Buddha, too, justified his mistrust of the pig by suggesting
that its corpulent body accommodated the souls of men
who in the previous life had sinned in thought, word and
deed. Buddhists, therefore, believe that pigs deserve the
disdain of honest men because they are the reincarnation of
the lowest humanity. When considered merely as an animal,
on the other hand, pigs are not regarded as evil; in fact,
Buddha himself, as we shall see later, awarded the pig a
privileged position in the Chinese calendar.

All things considered, however, it is hard to pretend that
God, in his numerous earthly guises, was particularly lenient

An English postcard depicting a family of pigs which appear to have made gluttony their philosophy of life. Opposite: a nineteenth-century jug, evidently designed for the dinner table.

towards the pig. Whether it was human or divine prejudice that was the root cause is a matter for debate, which only faith can resolve.

Back now to the land of Israel and the moment when Moses, coming down from Mount Sinai, denounced the race of swine. Time passed and, from all accounts, the pig did not fare any better. From the book of Proverbs comes one such example of the disdain with which pigs were treated. This book is a collection of sayings about all areas of life. They are reputed to be the fruit of the wisdom of the great King Solomon, collected and recorded by Ezra (fifth to fourth centuries B.C.). Proverbs gives a tremendous insight into the thoughts and beliefs of those times. The use of the pig in the disparaging analogy of this quotes reveals people's disregard for the "unclean" creature:

"Like a gold ring in a swine's snout
   is a beautiful woman without
   discretion."

Then, one day there appeared a man named Jesus, from the town of Nazareth, who was proclaimed the Son of God. At his birth he had been attended by an ox and an ass, revered by a flock of sheep and adored by three camels that had come from afar. But there was no sign, around his crib, of a pig. And for this absence, it had to pay dearly. Yet the pig had good reasons for hoping that its misfortunes would soon end. This Nazarene, who went about preaching good tidings, made a declaration which to his fellow Jews sounded revolutionary: "Not what goes into the mouth defiles a man, but what comes out of the mouth, this defiles a man." And he meant nothing, not even the flesh of the pig, even if the stubborn belief persisted that the pig itself was unclean.

This seemed to be the first step towards a general rehabilitation of the species: at the price of a triumphant return to the dinner table, the pig would no longer be regarded as a four-legged pariah.

Instead, there was a devastating reversal of fortune. In the country of the Gadarenes, Jesus met two men possessed by demons, who attacked him with bitter words. The meeting, witnessed by his disciples, occurred on the shores of the Sea of Galilee. Not far off, an enormous herd of swine was peacefully grazing. Disturbed by the presence of the Lord, the evil spirits that possessed the men spoke, thereby condemning the animals to renewed torment. "'If you drive us out,' they cried to Christ, 'send us into the swine, that we may enter into them.'" Jesus did not hesitate: he gave them permission and the demons "came out and went into the swine, and the whole herd rushed down the steep bank into the sea and perished in the waters."

Drowned, let it be said, even though the pig is a confident swimmer. The massacre was the death blow not only for that unhappy herd but also for all their descendants to come.

As the gospel episode strongly suggests, the Christian world, although accepting the pig as food, regarded the creature as the worthiest ally of Satan, who demanded to be accommodated in its gross body. More than ever, the pig came to be the very symbol of sin.

*This porcelain pig travelling bag is an
unusual early twentieth-century English
piggy bank, while the wooden pig, opposite,
with its unaccustomedly aggressive air and
exceptionally long tail, is Indonesian.*

In an unexpected stroke of religious retribution, the
Church of Rome would later represent the Jews gathered
inside the Temple in the guise of a sow suckling her piglets,
just as it was to depict its implacable fight against Judaism as
a duel in which the enemy, namely the Synagogue, is seen
astride a dirty black pig. And the same animal would be
featured in medieval iconography as the leader of those
who, being tainted by heresy, deserved to be burned at the
stake, first on earth, then in the hereafter.

The pig was thus charged by Beelzebub to drag man
down to the eternal flames of Hell. Ironic satisfaction,
perhaps, for a creature that has itself always been destined to
end up roasted.

Envoy of the gods and friend of the fairies

Strange as it may seem, the pig has two hearts. The first, absolutely ordinary and common to every living species, is the muscular organ that pumps blood through the body. The second, which hardly any other creature on earth possesses, is to be found at the end of the long, projecting muzzle, freely visible to all but noticed by few. It is the snout, which seen from the front has the typical shape of an upside-down heart, the tip pointed upward.

Perhaps it was after making this discovery that someone began looking at the pig as a magic animal, an attribution far removed from the much more usual and widespread allegation that it was essentially an unclean and filthy beast. And several cultures now came to regard it as a wonderful creature and thus beloved of the gods, a view supported by some other astounding characteristics. The gestation period of the sow, for example, is three months, three weeks and three days, a marvel for those who look for meanings in such coincidences – the perfect number repeated a perfect number of times. Then there is that unmistakable tail, curling in a spiral, an ancient symbol both of fertility and of

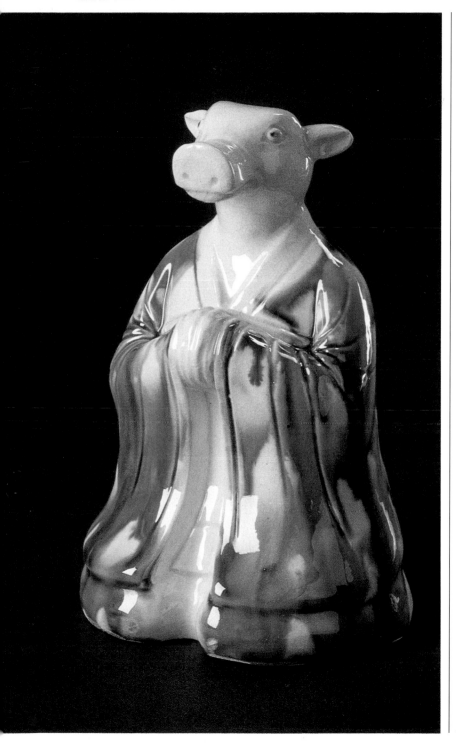

45

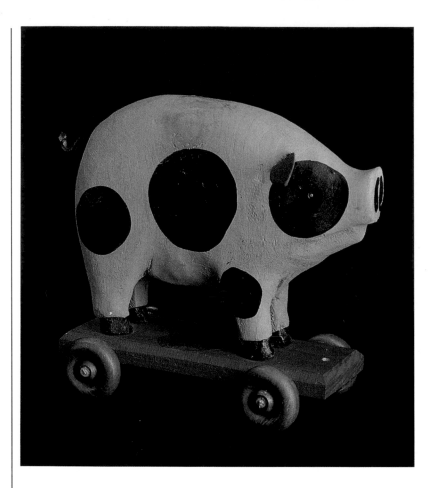

the travels of the soul after it leaves the body. In fact, the
Greeks and the Romans, people who considered the pig not
only tasty but also sacred, gave the creature an important
role in two fundamental stages of human existence: birth
and death.

It has to be said immediately, however, that not even the
pleasure of being accorded supernatural powers was
sufficient to save the pig from a cruel fate, for the animal was
now destined to end up with its throat cut on the altar, in
honour of one or other of the deities. Yet another irony.
The pig's long and historic journey of suffering was made
even more bitter by this strange contradiction of attitudes:
those who professed to hate it, like the Jews and the
Muslims, left it quietly alone, whereas those who regarded it

with love and honour, such as the Greeks and the Romans, could hardly be said to have treated it with particular kindness.

It could be, however, that there was a close, if subconscious, link between this love and the seemingly cruel end result. Indeed, from the dawn of Mediterranean civilization, prisoners taken in wars between tribes and neighbouring races were customarily offered as sacrificial victims to primitive gods. And there is evidence to suggest that many of these bloodthirsty rituals ended with horrible feasts in which the main dishes were the remains of the unfortunate men slaughtered on the altar. Moreover, considering that human flesh – as has been verified – has a pleasant taste and that neither the individual nor the community at large were as yet conscious of any taboo against cannibalism, there was a risk that religious ceremonies might end up transformed into abominable but well-established gastronomic traditions. Before this was allowed to happen, though, somebody discovered, perhaps accidentally, that the flesh of a pig tasted much like the flesh of a human being, so that the idea occurred: why not eat a pig instead of an enemy? The suggestion was obviously welcomed and thus *Homo sapiens*, thanks to some unknown cannibal, took a big step towards civilization.

From then on cannibalism was socially and culturally condemned. Generations to come would instinctively show gratitude and affection to the animal that, without their knowing it, had made such a contribution to human progress; and perhaps that was why it came to be considered sacred and dear to the gods. But for the animal itself, the whole thing was simply a gigantic swindle, and only centuries later was it to get some small measure of revenge.

In the Middle Ages, bands of assassins lurked in the

A papier-mâché piggy bank from Thailand. Opposite: a reproduction of a terracotta vase found in Pompeii. Following double page: a wooden rocking pig, also from Thailand.

woods and forests of central Europe, ambushing and killing wayfarers, cooking their flesh and selling it, by the pound, to the highest bidder. But because not even starvation could persuade people to eat human legs and ribs, these murderous rogues, evidently aware that the two types of meat tasted more or less alike, passed off their merchandise as pig flesh, thus making an easy sale. For one time in its history, the pig might have derived sadistic satisfaction from the fact that those who had always delighted in cooking and eating pork were now being served up themselves as dinner delicacies.

Let us go back, however, to ancient Greece, where after the pig had been proclaimed sacred, it was accorded quite an important position in religious and mythological traditions. The female was identified with the goddess Demeter, patroness of fertility and agriculture, who seemed neither surprised nor offended by being confused with a sow, but insisted on having a particularly plump specimen sacrificed to her at harvest time. So everything stayed in the family.

The pig also played a leading role in the Eleusinian mysteries, the most famous and obscure of all Greek religious rites, associated with the cult of Demeter herself, who was evidently convinced that the tribe of pigs was indebted to her. The goddess imposed on anyone wishing to be initiated into her secrets the explicit obligation of handing the priests a piglet, as an entry pass, which would then be slaughtered as a sign of expiation.

Even the handsome Apollo was content to use the pig for his own ends. When Orestes arrived at the temple of Delphi to ask pardon for having killed his treacherous mother, Clytemnestra, the god purified him by smearing him from head to foot with the blood of an unfortunate piglet which had been freshly slaughtered as representative of the entire tribe. For Jove and his relatives, it seems to have been no more than an amusing diversion to order priests, warriors,

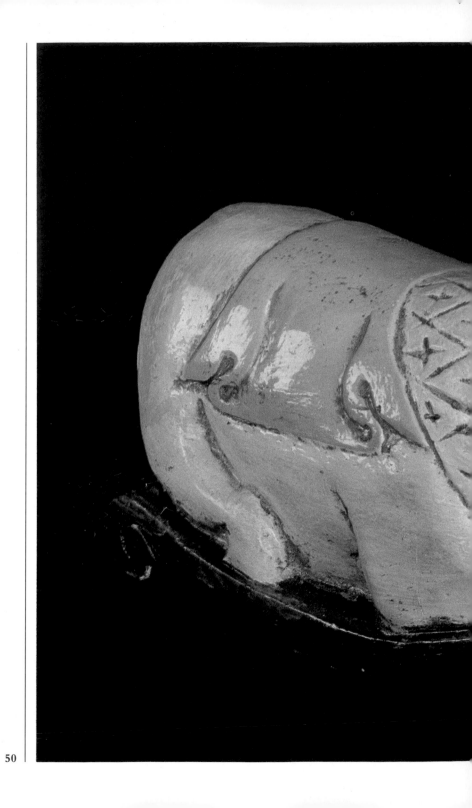

farmers and penitents to slit the throats of pigs in their name. Yet, as some consolation for the pig and repayment for all the spilt blood, the immortal gods did allow the creature certain extraordinary privileges: for example, they appointed it Olympian ambassador on Earth, expressly delegated to convey their incontestable will to mortals. Thus, when the devout Aeneas, returning from Troy, landed on the shores of Latium, the gods, in order to instruct him where to pitch his tents, sent him a sow with 30 piglets clinging to her teats.

The Trojan hero not only received the heavenly message but, persuaded that nothing was a matter of chance, attributed clear significance to the incredible number of sucklings and waited patiently for 30 years before setting out to found the city of Lavinia.

Given the dynastic relationship between Aeneas and the Latin people, it is evident that this anonymous sow

A group of pigs from Bali, where craftsmen carve unmistakable wooden pigs with huge, pointed ears and a curved back, often boldly portrayed coupling with one another.

contributed in her way to the foundation of the Eternal City, Rome itself, although history has chosen to blot out that fact and give credit, admittedly deserved, to the far more famous Capitoline wolf.

Despite this unforgivable oversight, the Romans genuinely venerated the pig. For one thing, they gave it a name, *maialis*, meaning dear to the goddess Maia to whom it was offered as a gift on the first of May, which, prior to becoming the feast of the workers, was the feast of the pigs. They heaped it with honours worthy of a Caesar.

Adopting the Greek principle whereby the animal was held to be sacred, they made it the rule not to mention its name. When they could not avoid referring to it, they followed it with a ritual phrase of apology. So they would say, "I have bought a pig, if you will excuse the expression," "My pig, if you will excuse the expression, is getting fat," or "My pig, if you will excuse the expression, is dead."

It is not hard to understand the reasons for this unusual delicacy in the choice of words. Once again the pig is compelled to play a double role and to endure that everlasting contradiction: the pagans are kindly disposed to it but always end up, albeit with the excuse of sacrificing it to the gods, by killing it and gorging on its flesh. Yet the cruel irony was that the creature grew up in a warm, loving atmosphere: every Roman family raised at least one pig, which was cosseted like any other household pet. But neither grief nor remorse prevented them, when the moment was ripe, from eating it in celebration of some feast or special occasion and even, as they made merry, inventing a new name for their favourite sow; only now, with its insides removed and stuffed with game, fruit and assorted delicacies, the poor animal bore more resemblance to the celebrated wooden horse, likewise packed with surprises, with which Ulysses breached the walls of Troy.

Even though they indulged themselves in orgies of feasting, in which the pig played a central, if passive role, the Romans continued to hold the animal in high esteem. To show their respect and consideration for the sow – symbol, as in Greece, of fertility and thus the patron of every birth – they also accorded her a special place in funeral ceremonies: she was given the sad task of accompanying the deceased person on his or her final journey. Ritual prescribed that, following a death, a sow should be slaughtered in order to purify the bereaved family. If the sacrifice took place in the presence of the corpse, it was called *praesentanea*; in the event of the body not being laid out in the home, it was known as *praecidanea*. In both cases, the animal's fate was the same.

An early twentieth-century trombone-playing pig from Bavaria. Opposite: a terracotta pig inspired by the Celtic legend in which the wizard, Merlin, was accompanied by a pig, here shown with its wizard's hat.

Supreme sacrifices of this kind were, in fact, commonplace; for virtually any act in the private or public life of Rome, ranging from a marriage contract to the ratification of an international treaty, could be sanctioned by the propitiatory killing of a pig. Thus almost any occasion was an excuse for cutting the creature's throat. Evidently, for the sons of Romulus, the blood of a pig carried the same expectations and hopes for good luck as would nowadays be attributed to a glass of sparkling champagne.

This bloodthirsty tradition whereby the pig is considered to be beloved of the gods and capable, through the act of sacrifice, of changing human fortunes for the better, is to be found, too, in many other cultures. For example, on the Indonesian island of Timor, whenever rain is needed for the fields, a black boar is slaughtered and offered to the Earth goddess, whereas if a period of calm weather is required, a white boar is similarly sacrificed. This is further proof of the remarkable nature of the pig which, among its countless other attributes, has magical powers, too, where climate is concerned.

There is also, of course, the famous episode in Greek legend in which the traveller Ulysses lands on the island of Aiaie and encounters the beautiful and mysterious sorceress, Circe. The treacherous woman, attracted to the sturdy Greek, endeavours to seduce him by turning all his companions into swine, evidently in the belief that such a guise is appropriate for the entire race of men. In the *Odyssey*, the astute hero manages to save the situation and restore his friends to their original shape. According to a later tradition, however, the Homeric story takes on a different significance as many of the Greeks, finding satisfaction in their newly acquired animal status, succeed in conveying to their leader, by means of persuasive grunts, the fact that they would prefer to be left in peace to live as pigs, a plea to which Ulysses agrees.

The transformation of men into swine, incidentally, is a common occurrence in the myths of other nations. Thus the ancient inhabitants of the Andaman Islands, in the Gulf of Bengal, believed that all pigs were descended from a metamorphosed man. The legend is that after the various animals on Earth, which did not yet include any omnivorous species, had finished feeding, there were still some leftovers. The Great Divinity decided that he needed to create a being with less finicky habits, which would consume literally everything. So he announced to humankind that he would reward the individual who presented himself first, running on all-fours and giving out the most repulsive cries. But it was a trick: for the prize

would be the credit for inventing the grunt and immediate transformation into a pig, with the obligation of devouring any kind of food that was offered from that time onward.

Still on the subject of metamorphosis, it is worth recalling the two nephews of Math, a mythical king of Wales, who were accused of high treason towards their uncle and were changed, by magic touch, into swine.

Then, too, there are those who transform themselves into pigs by their own free choice. This was the case with the elderly Chan, father of Lug, a demigod worshipped by the Celts, who disguised himself with snout, lard and all to flee from assassins, but who then decided to face cruel fate in his own guise, preferring death as a man to life as a pig.

Celtic mythology, more than any other, therefore assigns a central position to the role of the pig. Even its appearance on Earth is ascribed to a marvellous event: fairies, inhabitants of a luminous, enchanted kingdom gave the creature as a gift to human beings representing everlasting fertility and abundance.

Evidently aware of its magical origins, the Celtic pig tends to frequent places and consort with people worthy of its lineage: thus, it spends much time rooting for acorns beneath the oak, the most sacred of the forest trees, and was a constant companion of the Druids, mysterious individuals who mingled the vocations of priest and sorcerer, so that the creature thereby fulfilled the familiar dual role of pet and sacrifice. But as evidence of the extraordinary virtues of the animal, the fire in which it was roasted was destined never to die out and to fuel the oven for the festivities in the world to come.

A fat wooden pig, made in the United States. Opposite: apart from its original colours, this pig boasts another feature: the snout is a whistle in terracotta, following a tradition from the region of Apulia in Italy.

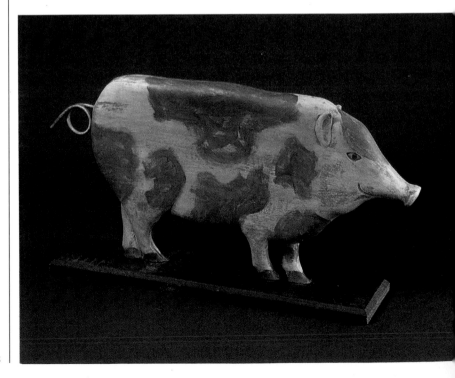

The most famous of all Celtic legends concerns the deeds of King Arthur and the Knights of the Round Table. Here the pig is in its element, though it must share the honours with its cousin, the wild boar, which is identified with the wizard Merlin, symbol of wisdom. In contrast, Arthur himself is the epitome of strength, represented by a bear. Nevertheless, it is the placid, pink farmyard pig that is so often depicted at Merlin's side, exhibiting a loyalty which the good wizard repays by choosing it as his constant companion when, according to one of the many versions, he decides to abandon the world of humans. Before this happens, however, the pig scores one of its most notable triumphs when, guided by its remarkable sense of smell, it roots about in the forest and finds none other than the Holy Grail, the mythical cup from which Jesus drank during the Last Supper. This epic quest has already been attempted, in vain, by brave and fearless knights such as Lancelot, Gawain, Bohort and Perceval, not to mention, centuries later, a rather less poetic but even more popular mythical hero named Dr Indiana Jones. None of them, however, possessed the singular aptitudes of our four-legged friend.

From hell to paradise with a saint

The patron saint of the pig is St Anthony The Abbot. Thanks to his protection, the animal that has for centuries been branded with the mark of infamy has not merely earned its merited rehabilitation in the eyes of the faithful but has also gained its right to enter into the House of God and to occupy a respected place there.

In Catholic churches all over the world, statues portraying the saint are often accompanied by figures of the pig, crouched affectionately and devotedly at the holy man's feet. This unusual association of the sacred and profane has long induced theologians and experts in religious matters to rack their brains in an attempt to comprehend how a man destined for glory in paradise could ever have been seen in the company, during his life, with a creature so unpopular in Heaven as to be considered in league with the Prince of Shadows himself. Although no decisive proof appears to have emerged from their learned studies and enquiries, they have concluded that this embarrassing relationship must have occurred because of the Devil's own sinister machinations. To understand how this happened, we have

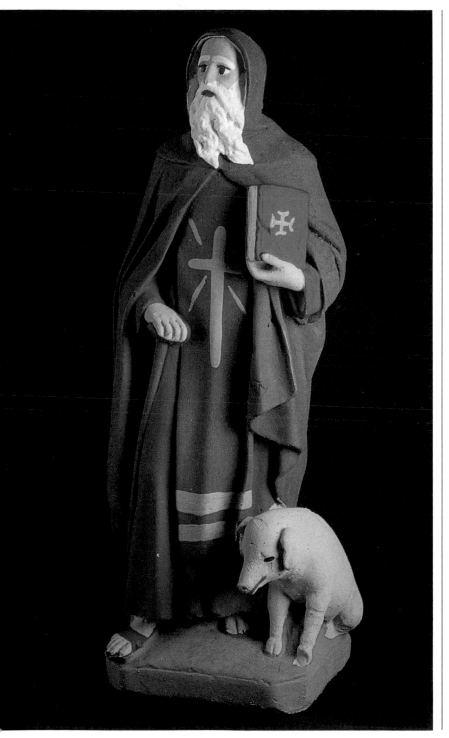

Above and opposite: two sows from Thailand, the first in ivory, the second, a kitchen glove, in cotton. Many objects in the shape of pigs are manufactured in the Far East, as the pig is one of the signs of the Chinese zodiac.

to know something about the background of the saint.

Anthony was born around A.D. 255 in a village not far from Heracleopolis, in Middle Egypt. Orphaned while still quite young, he sold all his family goods and retreated to the desert where he lived in absolute solitude for some twenty years, first taking up residence near an ancient tomb and later in an abandoned castle on the Nile, in the neighbourhood of Aphroditopolis. Here he devoted his life to meditation and prayer, and underwent a series of temptations. One of these involved his fateful encounter with the pig.

A hermit seeking to conduct a dialogue with God, far from civilized society, was clearly none too easy a victim for Satan, who chose to subject him to temptation rather than confront him directly. Thus the Devil, in an attempt to seduce the pious Anthony with the pleasures of sin and to torment him until he forsook his faith, appeared before him in a fleshly guise. The embodiment of his wicked schemes was, once again, the pig. The close links between this creature and eternal damnation was immediately evident to the future saint who, bemused by an onslaught of obscene and menacing grunts, wavered dangerously. Then, sustained by his unflinching faith, he summoned up his strength and managed to utter the formula of exorcism: "Get thee behind me, Satan!" The Devil, aroused to fury, belched flame, smoke and foul oaths, but was eventually put to flight, leaving the body he had temporarily taken over and abandoning it on the battlefield.

Freed of the unwelcome presence of its lodger, the pig proceeded to reveal its true nature: a harmless animal, confused by the turn of events and terrified of the hostile desert environment. Moreover, it had a real fear of being roasted on the spit of the hermit who, without knowing it, would thereby have been consigned to the everlasting flames of Hell. Anthony, however, was a good and saintly individual, incapable of acting from motives of simple revenge, and prepared to welcome, in a Christian spirit, the

NOUS
PORTONS BONHEUR

A French print showing the "Saint of pigs" and other tokens of luck. Opposite: spits surmounted by bronze pigs: the third on the right is Greek, the others are from Turkey. Pork, forbidden to Muslims, was introduced to Turkey when emigrants brought back eating habits from Germany.

unexpected guest which was content to curl up happily at his feet. It was in this manner that a bond was formed between man and beast, an association celebrated in sculpture and painting, where the pig deservedly occupies a place in the foreground as an incarnation of the temptations that can only be resisted, as Anthony did, by practicing asceticism. Such representations, in fact, are an allegorical celebration of the victory of Good, as portrayed by the saint, over Evil, in the transformed guise of the pig. In the Christian tradition of iconography, however, the identification of the swine and Satan gradually disappeared, so that the animal came to be depicted, not with the harsh and sinister features appropriate to a servant of the Devil, but with the soft and docile attributes of a pet: an animal surely incapable of the slightest degree of wickedness.

There are those, nevertheless, who contend that the transformation was itself the work of St Anthony. The creature sent into the desert to torture the Christian hermit with lustful temptations was actually a fierce, wild black boar that only changed shape after the hasty retreat of Satan,

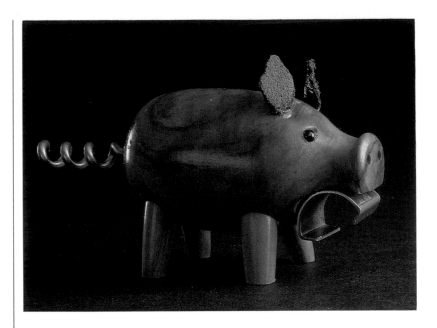

when it took on the guise of an inoffensive domesticated pig.

Throughout the Middle Ages, indeed, there was confusion between the two species, mainly because the pig, still dark in colour and often furnished with powerful tusks, much resembled its wild relation. Only in special circumstances was a clear distinction made. This happened to the pigs that, until the thirteenth century, had frequently been portrayed with pride on the shields of certain knights; now, suddenly, they found themselves ousted by wild boars.

The decision to make this change was taken, according to the chronicles, by warriors such as Guermond le Porc and Warnier Pourcel, men who, despite their pertinent names, felt that their bold soldierly image was hardly furthered by an association with a playful pig or chubby sow. So, not wishing to abandon the swine family altogether, they chose the fearsome boar as a new and more appropriate battle emblem. The reverse occurred, however, where representations of St Anthony were concerned, since the proper companion for the venerable old man was obviously an animal of suitably contrite and humble appearance: a wild boar was much too ferocious an associate for someone tranquilly immersed in prayer. In time, the excessively

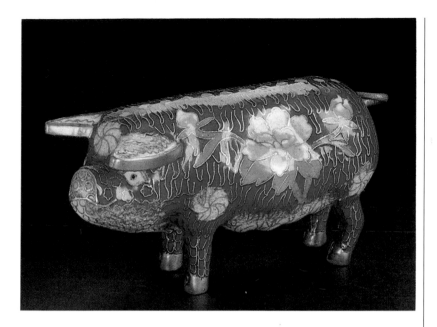

Traditional cloisonné *work involves attaching enamel to metal by a special technique. This floral sow is from Hong Kong. Opposite: a corkscrew-tailed pig from Ibiza.*

submissive nature of the pig helped to foster a second version of the meeting between the saint and the beast. Episodes, such as this one, evolved through Hispano-Arabic tales of the saint's life and have little basis of truth – in fact, St Anthony never left Egypt.

Anthony, on his way one day from Barcelona, suddenly heard heart-rending sobs coming from a farmyard. Going in to see what was happening, he came upon a sow which, by means of her desperate grunts, gave him to understand that one of her piglets, born lame, was dying. The saint, much moved, took the baby in his arms and, with a simple gesture of his hand, healed it immediately. The animal restored by this miracle, although risking its mother's disapproval, decided to follow its saviour everywhere. From that moment on, St Anthony was not only depicted with his travelling companion but was also recognized as the

protector of all domestic animals, with a particular concern, naturally, for the pig.

This heavenly recommendation brought considerable advantages to our friend the pig. The monks of St Anthony Abbot founded a religious order in France at the beginning of the eleventh century, known as the Hospital Brothers of St Anthony. These were pilgrimage centers for sufferers of ergotism, a common disease caused by eating the flour of grain poisoned by ergot. The hospitallers wore black robes with a Tau cross and went around asking for alms, accompanied, in the tradition of St Anthony, by a pig. Around the neck of the animal was hung a bell that announced from afar the arrival of this curious pair of mendicants. The charitable work of the monks won them favour with the people and eventually the pigs of this Order were allowed to roam freely in the streets and woods to feed. The Order of Hospitallers spread widely over western Europe and black-robed monks with their pigs and bells became a common sight in many parts.

As time passed, however, the pig won its independence and began to live quite freely outside the monastery precincts, realizing that it was more profitable to fend for itself. Separated from its human companion, therefore, the resourceful pig set out on its new mission, with the object not so much of seeking charity as of satisfying its immediate needs, in other words its appetite. The moment people heard the tinkling of the bell, they would bring out the food earmarked for the monks, leave it and retire indoors, as

A fine example of a pig in ivory. Opposite: an eighteenth-century Dutch print showing the East India Company being devoured by various kinds of animal, including the omnivorous pig. Preceding double page: a beautiful Chinese jade pig.

good manners demanded. But it was the rascally pig alone that would simply wander up, sniff, gobble up the titbits and beat a retreat, leaving the charitable householders none the wiser but with a clear conscience, happy in the knowledge that they had fulfilled their merciful Christian duty of providing food for the hungry. And, in a sense, this was true.

In any event, when the swinish trick was discovered, people, possibly as a sign of their devotion to the saint, continued to exhibit charity to the animals from the monasteries, now known familiarly as "St Anthony's pigs."

This porcelain shepherdess with one piglet in her arms and three more at her feet dates from the 1960s. According to old Chinese custom, the pig was a favourite pet of children and was second only to the dog in general popularity.

Right through the Middle Ages around western Europe, until a century or so ago, the animals enjoyed total immunity and privileged social status, rather like that of the sacred cows of India. They were licensed to roam freely through the streets around the monasteries, and no person, not even the poorest, dared consider them as the means of keeping starvation at bay.

Apart from the famous bell, these elite pigs were distinguished from ordinary pigs by a small notch on the ear, representing a cut made by the monks when the piglets were born. In France this tiny sign assumed such importance that it became a feature of general identification: the word "encoche," meaning "notch," evolved into "cochon." The animals were quite brazen in their importuning techniques and even learned how to butt their heads insistently against the house doors if they did not get what they wanted. Their identification with the saint whom they represented on Earth was transferred into popular folklore, so much so that in the Abruzzi, a region in central Italy, when someone had no food to offer the animal, they would shoo it off with the words: "Antuoò, vattènne," meaning "Be off with you, Anthony!"

The saint's popularity in the Middle Ages won him the title of patron saint of butchers, brush makers and grave diggers, and protector of hogs and other domestic animals. There is even a trace of his fame left in the English language: the word "tantony" is a diminuitive applied to pigs (smallest of the litter) and to bells (smallest of the peal).

At least for once, then, the pig managed to acquire a modicum of social standing and was not unavoidably condemned to end up in someone's stomach. Actually, as some scholars point out, the love for pigs displayed by the monks was tempered by a measure of self interest, although

72

in this case it was not a question of food so much as
philanthropy. The monks' interest in them arose from their
desire to cure the pestilence that was so rife in the twelfth
and thirteenth centuries. One of the symptoms was a skin
eruption which was interpreted by the religious brothers as
a manifestation of the Devil. Because they were followers of
the celebrated saint who had driven away Satan, the monks
felt they had a mission to heal the victims of this particular
complaint, which soon became known as "St Anthony's
fire." Since the condition was traditionally treated with

pig's lard, they began to raise the animals.

Many centuries before being given heavenly protection by St Anthony, the pig had been favoured by another divine individual. There is a Chinese tradition that Buddha, before he left the Earth, summoned all the animals. But only twelve creatures accepted his invitation, presenting themselves in this order: rat, ox, tiger, rabbit, dragon, snake, horse, sheep, monkey, rooster, dog and, last but not least, pig. As a reward for their interest, Buddha put each of them in charge of one year, from then on through the ages, and established that people born in various years should possess the psychological characteristics of the animal under whose sign they had come into the world. This was the origin of the Chinese horoscope in which "pigs" are seen as patient, fundamentally well balanced and well disposed towards others, though others often take advantage of their generosity. Moreover, they enjoy life's pleasures, as well as possessing cultural and artistic talents. In love they are loyal and sometimes ingenuous, which frequently brings disappointment, and they have an extremely sensuous nature. The year 1995 is a Year of the Pig: by subtracting twelve from this figure and checking back by dozens, it is possible to work out which years are protected by the pig. And anyone born in these years has the right to proclaim without embarrassment or shame: "I am a pig."

A picturesque piggy bank from Mexico, in terracotta and coloured wool: the handle on the back typifies the porcelain products of this craftsman. Opposite: a black pig mask from China.

Leipzig, 1920, and a child and a pig raise their glasses punctually at midnight to welcome the New Year. The postcard follows a German tradition, still prevalent, whereby marzipan pigs are given as good luck symbols for the coming year.

Bringer of luck, keeper of fortunes

Is the pig a lucky animal? From what we have described so far, the answer would seem to be "no," because no matter the historical circumstances or the environmental conditions, the creature has certainly had more bitterness than satisfaction from life. Yet man has chosen to link the animal indissolubly with good fortune, and sees it as one of the principal bringers of luck. So although it is no great privilege to be born a pig, the belief is by now widespread that to entrust the supervision of one's destiny to the animal is to ensure guaranteed success. The Germans are so convinced of this that they have come to use the word "Schwein," pig, as a synonym for "Glück," luck. And in many countries, especially of central Europe, it is traditional, on the first of January, to exchange marzipan piglets in augury of the following twelve months. For the Chinese, too, anyone born, according to the calendar divisions established by Buddha, under the sign of the pig, is blessed by destiny.

In fact, there is only one story in which swine are said to have brought bad luck to members of the human race. And

perhaps even this exceptional case would have passed unrecorded had it not concerned the heir to the throne of France. On 13 October 1131, Prince Philip, the thirteen-year-old eldest son of Louis VI ("The Fat"), was riding on horseback down the Rue Saint-Jean in Paris. Suddenly a huge pig came galloping out of a side alley and collided with the royal steed.

It is worth remembering, at this point, that in the twelfth century pigs were licensed to roam freely through the city and took advantage of this concession to look for food. This was mainly in the form of domestic refuse so at least they were performing a useful cleaning function. Crashing into young Philip's horse, this particularly reckless pig caused a

A terracotta piggy bank from Romania. Opposite: a curious early twentieth-century French ashtray, which shows a pig leaning on the four suits of a pack of cards, again a token of luck.

fatal accident: as he fell, the prince hit his head violently against the ground and died on the spot. The offending animal, a precursor of today's dangerous drivers, was never traced. In contemporary chronicles and reports the creature was described as "porcus diabolicus," not only because of the tragedy it had caused but also because of the disastrous dynastic repercussions the accident created.

In place of the unfortunate Philip, the king's younger son, Louis VII, ascended the throne, a delicate youth unfitted for royal duties. He weakened his country and was unpopular with his subjects who were of the opinion that this wretched pig, at any rate, had not brought good luck to anyone.

There is another pig associated with an unfortunate event, but it belongs to legend rather than history. The animal in question was called Big Bill, and its name is entered in the *Guinness Book of Records* as the fattest pig ever to have lived. In 1933 its owner, W.J. Chappell, intended to put it on show at the Chicago Fair, but the truck carrying the creature collapsed under the weight, causing a double

fracture of Mr Chappell's leg and convincing him that the time had come to get rid of the animal. So poor Big Bill was given an overdose of chloroform in a machine shop in Jackson, Tennessee. After the deed had been done, the pig's statistics were recorded: it weighed 182 stone (1,158 kg), stood 4½ ft (1.52 m) at the shoulder and measured almost 9 ft (3 m) in length. In recognition of these incredible physical attributes, the body was embalmed in a museum where the public gazed in admiration of it for years, while Mr Chappell, lamed for life, continued to curse the obese animal that had brought him bad luck.

Nevertheless, the exception proves the rule; and the rule honours the pig, not only at the dinner table but also in the realm of good fortune. So, alongside the centuries-old image of a morally unworthy creature (though much appreciated as food), the pig has more recently come to be seen as the symbol of comfort, prosperity and abundance. This is reflected by the "piggy banks" that children all over the world use to save up their pocket money and then break open with a hammer to spend the money in the nearest toyshop. It is a rite that, although bloodless, commemorates the flesh and bone sacrifice of the pig, stuffed with good things and then, poor thing, ripped to pieces.

It is anyone's guess as to who first got the bright idea of using the pig as a money box, but some would say it could be traced back, indirectly, to the distinguished French military engineer, Sébastien Le Prestre, Comte de Vauban (1633–1707). Although doubtlessly preoccupied with a thousand other more urgent matters, the versatile nobleman, who knew something of economics, must have risen from his bed one morning bothered by a quandary. If one had a certain amount of money, sufficient to buy an animal, and one only, what species should it be? We can never know the mental processes that induced the count to pose to himself this strange question, but his answer was unequivocal. The animal would have to be none other than our friend, the pig.

To reach this conclusion, Vauban had apparently set his sights on a pregnant sow and plunged into ridiculously convoluted calculations concerning the creature's reproductive capacity. With obsessive determination and mathematical preciseness, he worked out that in the course of ten years, this original female and her prolific descendants would give birth to 6,434,338 piglets, no more, no less.

It was clear, therefore, that the purchase of a pregnant sow must represent the most profitable of possible investments, at least in the sphere of animals. Impressed by this staggering statistic, the count's contemporaries decided that a creature capable of yielding such a high interest rate was eminently suitable as a model for teaching the rudiments of economics to the younger generation. Consequently, in due course, someone fashioned a pig in

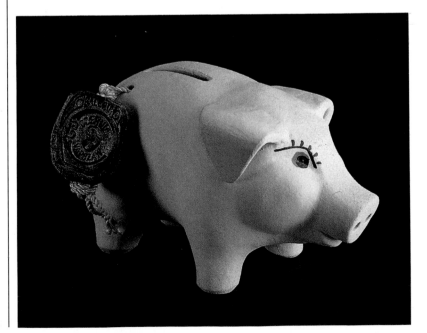

A plaster pig with a lock, made by a nineteenth-century German craftsman. Opposite: a piggy bank from a Warsaw workshop, as the attached seal of guarantee tells us.

terracotta to serve as a miniature strongbox for a child's modest savings. And this bringing together of pig and unglazed earthenware was in itself significant, for it united two old friends who went back as far as the beginning of time. It was, in fact, the pig that revealed to mankind the virtues of this material.

That, at any rate, is the argument supported by an ancient legend from the Ukraine, according to which an anonymous individual, preparing one day to feast on a plump little piglet, and wanting to ensure that it did not run away, placed it in a muddy hole until the fatal hour neared. The animal, perhaps unaware of what lay in store, made the most of its temporary abode and had a fine time rollicking in the mud, which was, in fact, clay. When the man pulled it out, he did not bother to clean it up and tossed it immediately into the fire for roasting. But then, while he was enjoying his meal, he became aware that the meat, despite being dirty and encrusted, tasted much better than

usual. And he realized, in a flash, that it was the enveloping earth that had made the pork so appetizing. What had been grasped by accident clearly deserved to be put to the scientific test. It was unnecessary to smear the food every time with mud; it simply had to be cooked in a container made of a mixture of clay and water, hardened in the flames. Terracotta had been discovered. Here was a fundamental step forward in the human journey. Once again the generous pig, unwittingly as ever, had played a determinant role. As partial consolation, it is worth pointing out that it was a decisive moment, too, for the pig's progeny. The creature had, in fact, learned the pleasures of rolling about in the mud, a pastime which was to give it a reputation of positively revelling in filth, whereas the truth is that it helped protect it from the heat of the sun and from the irritating activities of skin parasites. Although not commonly known, this is, in fact, the only reason why the pig deems it unwise always to maintain itself in a state of pristine cleanliness.

In Burma, there was another theory that held that the pig,

originally, was so clean as to be pure and spotless. Local people, it would seem, with not much of an eye for appearances, began to confuse the animal with the whitest figure in creation, namely the moon. By some enormous stretch of the imagination, the great ball in the night sky was no more nor less than a fat pig, feeding peacefully in the darkness. Even the observable fact that twice a month the moon dwindled in size, taking the form of a concave crescent, did nothing to change people's minds, for they simply explained it away by saying that these were the animal's canine teeth, the long tusks that the pigs had lost only comparatively recently, after becoming fully domesticated. The whole thing would have remained a harmless fantasy had it not been for a desperate, starving hunter who, one night, aimed his poisoned arrow at the animal floating over the black horizon, intending to kill it and eat it. Angered by this outrage, the white creature then decided to reveal its real identity – no ordinary member of the race of swine but the Moon itself, not just a heavenly body to be admired but a powerful, and decidedly irritable,

This German bronze pig from the early part of the twentieth century stands confidently and cheerfully upright. Opposite: a garlanded Italian porcelain pig from the 1920s. Preceding double page: a delightful and lively group from the Saltford Pottery in England, which specializes in pig objects.

divinity. Although the arrow had hardly registered a
pinprick, she reacted furiously and violently, tearing the
head of the unfortunate hunter clean from his body. Then,
tired of always being mistaken for a pig, she decreed that
henceforth all possibility of confusion must be eliminated,
commanding her "twin" to take on a different guise, no
longer white but thoroughly dirty. From then on, according
to the legend, every pig worthy of the name rolled
enjoyably in filth.

It is a moot question, therefore, whether the pig's passion
for mud derives from the discovery of a greedy Ukrainian,
the fantasy of a myopic Burman or, more mundanely, its
own free choice. What really counts is the excessive
importance that mankind has attributed to this swinish
foible, so that the pig and dirt are virtually synonymous. But
an occasional wallow in the mire should not be taken as in
any way indicative of other natural inclinations; the dirt is all
on the surface, not in the mind. There is no proof, for
example, that pigs are in any sense sexual athletes, in a
continual state of erotic excitement. On the other hand,
they cannot be denied feelings. Admittedly, they may not
be the most romantic of Nature's creatures, and a grunt is
not as pleasing – to the human ear, at least – as a purr or a
chirp; but there is evidence to suggest that they can be
touched by the pangs of love, as is demonstrated in a story
told by Gilbert White, the English naturalist, in 1789. It
concerns a fine sow who was attracted to a sturdy boar on a
nearby farm. When she felt the mating urge, she made
boldly for her destination, pushing her way through gates
after unlatching the wooden bolts with her snout. Not all
sows are necessarily so single minded when it comes to

affairs of the heart, but the tale does perhaps have a moral, none too flattering, if we care to apply it. When it comes to sexual behaviour, humans often act more like pigs than pigs do themselves.

One explanation for this confusion of roles comes from the Marìnd-Anìm, a tribe from New Guinea, who relate how, in ancient times, sows gave birth to children and women to piglets, to the great consternation of local midwives. After each happy event, the traditional enquiry, "Is it a boy or a girl," had to be modified to "Is it a human or a pig?" And so, in due course, a new, mixed race appeared, that of the Half-Pigs, creatures that belonged neither to the human or the swine species but that could pass from one to the other at will.

The split between the two races occurred after blood had been spilt. The Half-Pig Nazr adopted a piglet born to a woman and, because it was not the male duty to rear the young, he handed them over for safekeeping to two female friends named Sangan and Samaz. The baby, who was actually another Half-Pig, grew up and fell desperately in love with his foster-mothers. But because he could not hope to win their favours in the guise of a pig, he transformed himself one night into a charming youth and seduced them both. There then began a passionate three-way relationship that would have continued quite happily had not the mother of the girls become suspicious, noticing her daughters' unusual behaviour, and spied on them, discovering the whole affair. The indignant woman denounced the Half-Pig to the community, and he was condemned to death, the statutory punishment for all Half-Pigs who coupled with human beings. Nazr, his adoptive father, was himself ordered to execute the young lover, and though well disposed towards his Half-Pig, was unable to avoid the sad and terrible obligation. His eyes misty with

No dirt on this pig, which is obviously not averse to soap and water. Opposite: a pig-sock for hanging over the fireplace at Christmas.

tears, his mind in turmoil, he thrust a knife into the animal's body and let out an inhuman cry. Hearing it, the gods looked down from above and took pity on his plight. Thanks to their intervention, the gush of blood that issued from the belly of the pig rose up to the clouds and changed into a rainbow. And while Nazr gazed on the splendid colours in the sky, the storm in his heart died down. From that day, the appearance of the rainbow announced to the world the end of every storm. And in order to avoid a repetition of such dramas, mankind was henceforth distinguished from swine, while the race of Half-Pigs disappeared.

Commemorating this event, a wedding tradition is still observed in New Guinea whereby every girl of marriageable age raises a piglet which, on the morning of the ceremony, her future husband must bring to the altar and kill. Nevertheless, the extinction of the Half-Pigs and the clear separation of humans and swine did not prevent certain customs of the one from being attributed to the other, and vice versa. This explains, according to the Marind-Anìm, why pigs still get accused of excessive vices that are more typical of humans.

Legends of other cultures show the pig in a different light,

The cover of a French magazine and, opposite, a Russian peasant doll with pigs under either arm. Preceding double page: the blue and green pigs and the pig on the far left are Mexican, the fattest one is Hungarian, and the four others in front, from left to right, from Peru, Brazil, the USA and Austria.

but the end result is usually the same. The ancient Papuans, for example, to console a mother who had lost her child, would send her a piglet which it was her right and duty to rear as her own flesh and blood, even suckling it at the breast. In due course this custom assumed far more dramatic connotations, because every firstborn child was automatically exchanged for the last piglet born in the village. And although the human mother, given suitable inducement, might bring up the pig with loving care, the sow's maternal instincts only went so far: and thus the infamous habit of sacrificing the firstborn led to a succession of innocent deaths, given that the babies were mistaken, by their foster-mothers, for succulent morsels. Fortunately, the dreadful custom was abandoned centuries ago.

The truth is that a battle on their behalf would not be a popular cause. After all, how many of us would really be prepared to give up the pleasures that pigs, at the price of their life, bring to our tables? Possibly only those few who are not blinkered by enticing images of bacon or ham and who possess enough humility of mind to echo the *mea culpa* penned by Guy of Dampierre, count of Flanders, in his *Encyclopedia of French Agriculture*: "I would like to see the pig raised from the abject condition assigned to it by prejudice and ignorance, and given the respect it deserves." Unfortunately, that wish still remains a utopian dream. It will be a long time before calling someone a pig is taken as a delightful compliment and the animal itself spared the indignity of being cursed and reviled, or, even worse, being sacrificed to our gluttony. We who wish the creature well can only hope that the day will come when the pig, after so many centuries of cruel treatment, will assert the revolutionary spirit that undoubtedly lurks within. Then it will proclaim its total identity with the two-footed race

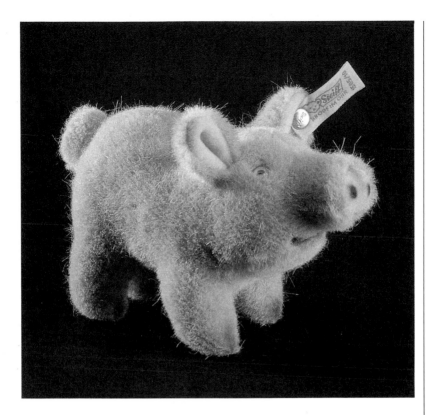

which has always exploited it. And in this context the final
words of George Orwell's *Animal Farm* take on the weight
of a biblical prophecy: "No question, now, what had
happened to the faces of the pigs. The creatures outside
looked from pig to man, and from pig to man again; but
already it was impossible to say which was which."

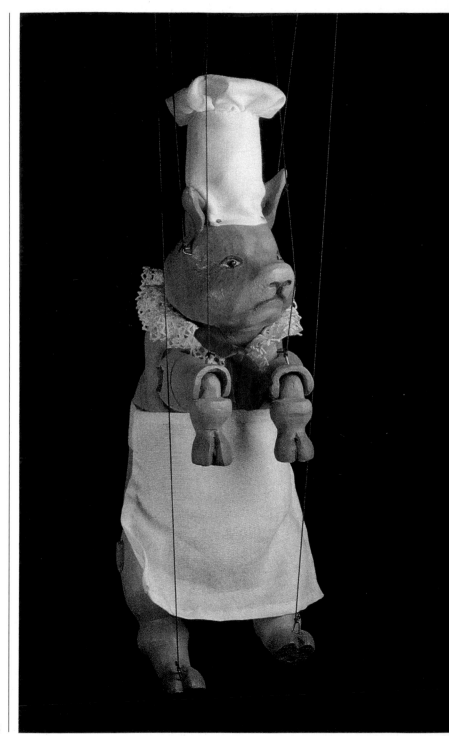

Prose, poetry and pigs

For those who are genuinely interested in the pig as an animal in its own right and not just as a tasty morsel laid out for display in a butcher's window or neatly packaged on the supermarket shelf, there are plenty of opportunities to become further acquainted in libraries and bookshops. Novelists, essayists and poets, some of them with greater literary skills than others, have, with commendable open-mindedness and insight, ventured beyond the customary bounds of prejudice and ignorance to celebrate the moral qualities of the pig; and the following extracts from a selection of better known works provide a good cross-section.

The pig features prominently in the world's literature but often, unfortunately, in a passive and unwelcome role, such as the centerpiece of a feast. This entertaining wooden puppet turns the tables – rather than being cooked, he will be doing the cooking.

LEWIS CARROLL, Alice in Wonderland

The metamorphosis of human beings into pigs is a fairly recurrent theme in mythology, fairy tale and fiction through the centuries, all over the world. The most famous example is perhaps that passage in the Odyssey in which Homer describes how the companions of Ulysses were transformed into swine by the sorceress, Circe. More familiar to children, however, is the mishap that befalls Alice during her amazing adventure in Wonderland, when she takes the Duchess's baby in her arms and is astonished to find it turning into a pig.

The baby grunted again, and Alice looked very anxiously into its face to see what was the matter with it. There could be no doubt that it had a *very* turn-up nose, much more like a snout than a real nose; also its eyes were getting extremely small for a baby: altogether Alice did not like the look of the thing at all. "But perhaps it was only sobbing," she thought, and looked into its eyes again, to see if there were any tears. No, there were no tears. "If you're going to turn into a pig, my dear," said Alice, seriously, "I'll have nothing more to do with you. Mind now!" The poor little thing sobbed again (or grunted, it was impossible to say which), and they went on for some while in silence.

Alice was just beginning to think to herself, "Now, what am I going to do with this creature when I get it home?" when it grunted again, so violently, that she looked down into its face in some alarm. This time there could be *no* mistake about it: it was neither more nor less than a pig, and she felt that it would be quite absurd for her to carry it any further.

So she set the little creature down, and felt quite relieved to see it trot away quietly into the wood. "If it had grown up," she said to herself, "it would have made a dreadfully ugly child: but it makes rather a handsome pig, I think." And she began thinking over other children she knew, who might do very well as pigs....

Below, a ceramic card holder of the 1930s, made in America, flanked by three inquisitive pigs. Opposite: a postcard illustrating a German fairy tale which tells of a luminous pig that appears mysteriously to certain children.

HANS CHRISTIAN ANDERSEN, **Fairy Tales**

The piggy bank plays a role in one of the tales of the great Danish story-teller. Here he portrays it as so full of itself that it does not realize the risk it runs of falling, with disastrous results.

The money-pig was stuffed so full that it could no longer rattle, which is the highest state of perfection to which a money-pig can attain. There he stood upon the cupboard, high and lofty, looking down upon everthing else in the room. He knew very well that he had enough inside him to buy up all the other toys, and this gave him a very good opinion of his own value.

The proud china piggy bank ends up smashed into a thousand pieces on the floor, and is substituted on the shelf by another piggy bank, this time with an empty stomach.

Below: an illustration from the early part of
this century. Opposite: a cloth pig of the
1920s.

TRADITIONAL POEMS AND DITTIES

*The pig also features in the famous collection of tales by the Brothers Grimm. Perhaps one
of the most popular pig tales of all is The Three Little Pigs. In this sad story, two little
pigs are gobbled up by the wolf who "huffs and puffs and blows the house down."
Fortunately, the third pig has the sense to build a house of bricks, and then traps the wolf
into coming down the chimney, straight into the soup pot.*

*Pigs assume a variety of roles in the many poems and ditties that have been handed
down through the ages. The origins of the following rhymes are probably lost in time, but
they all reveal the special place enjoyed by the pig in rural society, a feeling which is not so
strong in the modern quotes.*

THE LADY AND THE SWINE

There was a lady loved a swine,
  Honey, quoth she,
Pig-hog wilt thou be mine?
  Hoogh, quoth he.

I'll build thee a silver sty,
  Honey, quoth she,
And in it thou shalt lie.
  Hoogh, quoth he.

Pinned with a silver pin,
  Honey, quoth she,
That thou may go out and in.
  Hoogh, quoth he.

Wilt thou have me now,
  Honey? quoth she.
Speak or my heart will break.
  Hoogh, quoth he.

A PRETTY WENCH

I am a pretty wench,
  And I come a great way hence,
And sweethearts I can get none:
  But every dirty sow
  Can get sweethearts enough,
And I pretty wench can get none.

GRIG'S PIG

Grandfa' Grig
  Had a pig,
In a field of clover;
  Piggy died,
  Grandfa' cried,
And all the fun was over.

103

PATRICIA HIGHSMITH, **The Animal-Lover's Book of Beastly Murder**

Although fat and apparently lazy, pigs seem so good that they might well be mistaken for stupid. But never be tempted to think they will not lose their temper. That is a lesson learnt by M. Emile, a farmer who went out hunting for truffles with Samson, his prize boar, who one day was foolish enough to give it a kick. It was a fatal error, for the animal took swift revenge by killing him.

The awful pink and damp nose of the pig was almost in Emile's face, and he recalled from childhood many pigs he had known, pigs who had seemed to him as gigantic as this Samson now crushing the breath out of him. Pigs, sows, piglets of all patterns and colouring seemed to combine and become this one monstrous Samson who most certainly – Emile now knew it – was going to kill him, just by standing on him. The fork was out of reach. Emile flailed his arms with his last strength, but the pig wouldn't budge. And Emile could not gasp one breath of air. Not even an animal any longer, Emile thought, this pig, but an awful, evil force in a most hideous form. Those tiny, stupid eyes in the grotesque flesh! Emile tried to call out and found that he couldn't make as much noise as a small bird.

PELHAM GRENVILLE WODEHOUSE, **Summer Lightning**

How satisfying it is to raise a fat pig. So thought Sir Clarence, ninth earl of Emsworth, who was delighted to see his most aristocratic sow, aptly named Empress of Blandings, grow to an enormous size. So envious were his neighbours that the portly pig was the object of a sensational theft, around which all the events in this amusing novel revolve.

Lord Emsworth's mild eyes beamed. They always did when that noble animal, Empress of Blandings, was mentioned. The ninth Earl was a man of few and simple ambitions. He had never desired to mould the destinies of the State, to frame its laws and make speeches in the House of Lords that would bring all the peers and bishops to their feet, whooping and waving their hats. All he yearned to do, by way of ensuring admittance to Engand's Hall of Fame, was to tend his prize sow, Empress of Blandings, so sedulously that for the second time in two consecutive years she would win the silver medal in the Fat Pigs class at the Shropshire Agricultural Show. And every day, it seemed to him, the glittering prize was coming more and more within his grasp.

Earlier in the summer there had been one breathless sickening moment of suspense, and disaster had seemed to loom. This was when his neighbour, Sir Gregory Parsloe-Parsloe, of Matchingham Hall, had basely lured away his pig-man, the superbly gifted George Cyril Wellbeloved, by the promise of higher wages. For a while Lord Emsworth had feared lest the Empress, mourning for her old friend and valet, might refuse food and fall from her high standard of obesity. But his apprehensions had proved groundless. The Empress had taken to Pirbright, George Cyril's successor, from the first, and was tucking away her meals with all the old abandon. The Right triumphs in the world far more often than we realise.

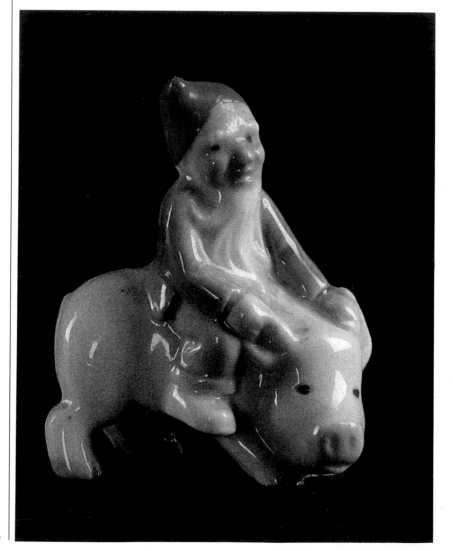

Pigs are patient types: the one below, a nineteenth-century example from Scandinavia, carries a gnome on its back; the one in the print opposite, dating from 1871, is apparently taking lessons from the swineherd, who seems to be teaching it to play the pipe.

THIS LITTLE PIGGY, **Traditional nursery rhyme**

In this famous nursery rhyme, played as a game at bathtime, pigs and piglets are identified with the pink chubby toes of babies. The toes of one foot are introduced as the five little piggies of the nursery rhyme. Starting with the big toe, the rhyme works to a climax – the role of the little toe is a little piggy who ran all the way home squealing, so the child is tickled accordingly from toe to head! Here, we have a refreshingly affectionate view of pigs.

> This little piggy went to market,
> This little piggy stayed at home,
> This little piggy had roast beef,
> This little piggy had none,
> And this little piggy went, "Wee! Wee! Wee!"
> All the way home.

Below: the Three Little Pigs, as brought to life by Walt Disney in 1933, fortunate survivors in their adventures with the Big Bad Wolf. Opposite: a myth from film history, no other than the young James Dean, here posing proudly beside a splendid champion pig.

MILAN KUNDERA, **The Unbearable Lightness of Being**

Who said that the dog is man's best friend? It was surely someone who did not know the qualities of the pig, an animal only too happy to fetch and carry and to show as much obedience and loyalty as Fido, expecting only a little love and a daily meal in return. Take, for example, the pig Mefisto, adopted by the main characters in this novel, Tereza and Tomàs. It proves to be an unusual pig and even makes friends with the dog Karenin, an unlikely friendship in any other circumstances.

The collective farm chairman became a truly close friend. He had a wife, four children, and a pig he raised like a dog. The pig's name was Mefisto, and he was the pride and main attraction of the village. He would answer his master's call and was always clean and pink; he paraded about on his hoofs like a heavy-thighed woman in high heels.

When Karenin first saw Mefisto, he was very upset and circled him, sniffing, for a long time. But he soon made friends with him, even to the point of preferring him to the village dogs. Indeed, he had nothing but scorn for the dogs, because they were all chained to their doghouses and never stopped their, silly unmotivated barking. Karenin correctly assessed the value of being one of a kind, and I can state without compunction that he greatly appreciated his friendship with the pig.

Household words the world over

Brief glossary of pigs in four languages

English

pig *n.* (from medieval *pigge*) a non-ruminant mammal of the family Suidae ‖ (*fig.*) a greedy, dirty, self-centered person ‖ (*slang*) policeman ‖ *eat like a pig, make a pig of oneself*, eat excessively ‖ *pigs might fly*, a highly unlikely occurrence ‖ *carry pigs to market*, try to do business ‖ *bring one's pigs to the wrong market*, make a bad deal ‖ *buy a pig in a poke*, buy or do something riskily, without prior consideration ‖ *pigheaded*, obstinate, stubborn.

pig *v.i.* to produce pigs ‖ (*slang*) to eat quickly, gulp down ‖ *pig it*, to live in wretched, squalid surroundings, as in a pigsty ‖ *pig out*, to overindulge in eating.

French

cochon *n.* (probably from *encoche*, tag for marking a pig) pig ‖ (*fig.*) *sale comme un cochon*, filthy as a pig ‖ *manger comme un cochon*, eat excessively, like a pig ‖ *tête de cochon*, pigheaded, stubborn person ‖ *nous n'avons pas gardé les cochons ensemble*, don't be so familiar! ‖ *jouer un tour de cochon à q.* play someone a dirty trick ‖ *un temps de cochon*, foul weather.

cochon *adj.* dirty, filthy, lascivious ‖ *histoire cochonne*, smutty story.

cochonner *v.i.* to produce pigs; *v.t.* to soil, botch, bungle.

Sometimes revenge is sweet: here are the three pigs again, feasting on the flesh of the wicked wolf, whose tail hangs out of the pot.

Italian

maiale *n.* (from Latin *maialis*) originally the castrated male destined for fattening; now used generally for any kind of pig || (*fig.*) person who does or says obscene things || *mangiare come un maiale*, eat excessively and greedily || *grasso come un maiale*, extremely fat || *sudicio come un maiale*, very filthy.

porco *n.* (from Latin *porcus*) a pig || flesh of a slaughtered pig, pork || (*fig.*) person who says or does obscene, revolting or dishonest things || awful, horrible; used as exclamations of indignation, disappointment or anger: *porco cane!*, *porco mondo!*, *porca miseria!* || *gettar le perle ai porci*, cast pearls before swine, give valuable things to those who do not deserve them || *fare i propri porci comodi*, behave in a self-centered manner || *cani e porci*, derogatory term for a random group of worthless individuals.

troia *n.* (from Latin *troia*, perhaps from *porcus troianus*, stuffed pig), sow || (*fig.*) woman of low habits, slut, bitch.

German

Schwein *n.* (from Germanic *swina*, from Latin *suinus*) pig || (*fig.*) dirty, filthy || (*pop.*) luck, fortune || *Armesschwein*, poor devil || *wie ein Schwein bluten*, bleed like a stuck pig || *das falsche Schwein schlachten*, make an irreparable error || *fett wie ein Schwein*, fat as a pig || *fressen wie ein Schwein*, eat excessively || *kein Schwein*, no one, not even a dog || *davon hat kein Schwein etwas gesagt*, nobody mentioned it || *kein Schwein kümmert sich darum*, nobody is interested in it || *Schweine werden auch vom Dreck fett*, everything helps.

Schweinegeld *n.* heaps of money || *ein Schweinegeld verdienen*, make lots of money.

Schweineglück *n.* outrageous luck.

Schweinehund *n.* swineherd's dog || (*vulg.*) dirty beast || *Der innere Schweinehund*, baseness, cowardice.

Acknowledgements

This book would not have been possible without the contributions of many pig enthusiasts and their collections.

The authors would like to thank the owners of the objects photographed, and the following:
Maurizio Epifani (L'oro dei farlocchi, Milan), Anna Giorgetti, Maria Laura Giovagnini, Aglaia Lovetti, Gioia Maselli, Luigi Sapino (Galleria Mirabilia, Turin), Giuliana Scotti, Stefano Vaj.

The publisher thanks Gruppo Mantero for allowing the reproduction of the Interseta design on the cover.

Pages 36 and 37: wooden pig by Giorgio Broglio, Val d'Aosta.
Page 57: terracotta pig by Ceilt Siopa, Milan.
Page 59: unique piece by Anna Panareo.
Page 99: pig-puppet by the Colla company, Milan.

Extract from Patricia Highsmith *The Animal Lover's Book of Beastly Murder* is reproduced by kind permission of Warner Books, Inc.

Quote on page 108 from *The Unbearable Lightness of Being* by Milan Kundera, copyright © 1984 by Harper & Row, Publishers, Inc., published by HarperCollins.

Picture sources

The pigs illustrated in this book belong to the following collections:
Franco Bonera (pp. 2, 8, 9, 10, 11, 16–17, 19, 20, 24, 25, 27, 28, 29, 33, 34, 36–37, 42, 43, 46, 48, 50–51, 54, 57, 59, 62, 63, 64, 66, 67, 71, 75, 78, 82, 84–85, 90, 92–93, 97);
Cristina Gerruti and Renato Favaron (cover, pp. 14, 21, 30, 38, 41, 49, 52, 61, 65, 68–69, 70, 73, 77, 80, 83, 86, 95, 98, 100, 102, 104, 105, 106, 107, 109);
Emilio Gargioni (p. 58);
Franco Marbelli (pp. 45, 55, 74, 79, 87, 88, 91, 94, 101);
Maria Portesan (pp. 13, 31, 32, 40);

All photographs by Giorgio Coppin in collaboration with Anna Giorgetti.